APPARATUS

Don McKay

M&S

Canadian Cataloguing in Publication Data

McKay, Don, 1942-
   Apparatus

Poems.
ISBN 0-7710-5763-6

I. Title.

PS8575.K28A86 1997   C811'.54   C96-932211-9
PR9199.3.M34A86 1997

The publishers acknowledge the support of the Canada Council and the Ontario Arts Council for their publishing program.

Typesetting by M&S, Toronto

Printed and bound in Canada

McClelland & Stewart Inc.
The Canadian Publishers
481 University Avenue
Toronto, Ontario
M5G 2E9

   2 3 4 5   01 00 99 98

For Jan

CONTENTS

I

TO SPEAK OF PATHS

The wolf at the door
and the wolf in the forest and the work
work work of art. The scrape,
the chop, the saw tooth
tasting maple. The cradle, the cup, the muscle
in your mother's arm and back
and pelvis, muscle flexing in the air
between two people arguing,
two people loving, muscle
pumping blood. Gut
summoned to speak. The rotary cuff, the wrist,
having learnt the trick of witching wands and locks,
the heft, the grain, the web,
the rub of moving parts.
And the tiny sea in the ear
and the moth wing in the mind, which wait.

TWINFLOWER

What do you call
the muscle we long with? Spirit?
I don't think so. Spirit is a far cry. This
is a casting outward which
unwinds inside the chest. A hole
which complements the heart.
The ghost of a chance.

*

Then God said, ok let's get this show
on the road, boy, get some names
stuck on these critters, and Adam,
his head on the ground in a patch of tiny
pink-white flowers, said
mmn, just a sec.
He was, let's say,
engrossed in their gesture,
the two stalks rising, branching, falling back
into nodding bells, the fading arc
that would entrance Pre-Raphaelites and basketball.
Maybe he browsed among the possibilities of elves.
Maybe he was blowing on the blossoms,
whispering whatever came into his head, I have
no way of knowing what transpired
as Adam paused, testing his parent's
limit, but I know
it matters.

*

Through the cool woods of the lower
slopes, where the tall
Lodgepole Pine point
into the wild blue while they supervise
the shaded space below, I walk,
accompanied by my binoculars and field guides.
I am working on the same old problem,
how to be both
knife and spoon, when there they are, and maybe have been
all along, covering the forest floor: a creeper, a shy
hoister of flags, a tiny lamp to read by, one
word at a time.

                  Of course, having found them, I'm about
to find them in the field guide, and the bright
reticulated snaps of system will occur
as the plant is placed, so, among the honeysuckles,
in cool dry northern woods from June to August.
But this is not, despite the note of certainty,
the end. Hold the book open,
leaf to leaf. Listen now,
Linnaea Borealis, while I read of how
you have been loved –
with keys and adjectives and numbers, all the teeth
the mind can muster. How your namer,
Carolus Linnaeus, gave you his
to live by in the system he devised.
How later, it was you,
of all the plants he knew and named,
he asked to join him in his portrait.
To rise in your tininess,
to branch and nod beside him
as he placed himself in that important
airless room.

Attention, always looking,
comes upon its home place.
Something shifts
in its tectonics, as if distance
simply took it in, eluding and embracing with the same
grand gesture. Sleep lies down
with concentration, concentration
sleep.
The British Museum sheds its charm.
Our faithful cravings,
muted like undesirable commercials,
translate themselves as fresh intensities of sky
which we inhale.
Whatever happens here, amplified,
fanged,
will be another sort of theatre.
The Varied Thrush,
floating a quavering
equivocal note,
says so.

> ". . . c'est le moment de parler de vous, chemins qui vous
> effacez de cette terre victime."
>
> — Yves Bonnefoy

One gestures to a blue
fold in the hills, meaning
follow your heart. Another scrawls
follow your nose into the raspberry canes
and may later show itself to be
the deer's own way to the water.
Some will speak
only to the third and fourth ears that persist,
vestigially, in the feet.
One way or another
they feed us a line, and we go,
dithering over the outwash or angled as an oar
into the forest, headed for the top,
the lake, the photo
opportunity, the grave of the trapper
who lived all alone and trained a moose
to pull his sleigh.
Strange marks on a far slope turn out,
hours later, to have been your zigzag path ascending,
earning every inch the waterfall beside it spends
like a hemorrhage. And always
the thrill of the pause, when your eye drinks
and your heart pounds and your legs
imagine roots, when your whole life,
like a posse, may catch up with you and tumble

headlong into the moment.
You may wish to say something to it, but your tongue
seems to be turning to an alder twig
and you must wait for wind.

not along with the music, which isn't listening,
but to the animal inside the instrument,
muffling the perfections of hammer, pedal,
wire, the whole
tool-kit, humming
he furs the air,
paints an exquisite velvet painting of a far-off country
where the rain falls
contrapuntally the wind lies on the land
like a hand caressing a cat's back, humming
"this is your death, which is but a membrane away,
which is but a leaf, turning,
which is falling in these delicate
explicit fingers, as you have always known,
and worn, though only we,
the instrumentalists,
have found a way to sing it for you.
Sleep."

CHICKADEE ENCOUNTER

ok ok ok ok
here they come, the tidbits, the uppers,
animating the bramble,
whetting details. Hi,
I always say, I may be glum or dozy, still
hi, how's it going, every time they zip –
drawing that crisp invisible lilt from point to point – up
to check me out: ok: it's practically pauseless,
but as though some big machine –
domestication maybe – hiccuped,
a glitch through which the oceanic
thirsts of poetry pour: o
zippers, quicklings,
may you inherit earth, may you
perch at the edge of the shipwreck of state,
on the scragged uneconomical alders,
and chat.

A smooth unhurried
gulp: and the lake
has swallowed the duck
                    Being left
so suddenly, without benefit of flight paths teaching
distance to the eye, stretching the muscle
it drinks with, you tend to think of crossings-over,
metamorphoses, you tend to hold your breath,
which is a bad idea. In the *Kalevala*, this
is ocean's last eternal moment, during which the Goldeneye
brings bottom to the top, the mirror
puckers up and speaks, and land,
with its metabolism of true-life adventure,
starts.
Absence makes the heart grow.
And the reappearance,
always expected, always,
like a burp
            surprises.
                    There it is
beside the reed bed, wearing the same
misshapen moon, the gold eye glaring.
Was it stricken by a glimpse
of something awful on the other side? Or,
unbeknownst to us, or to the *Kalevala*, has some hot star
seized upon that lens to stare into our atmosphere, furious
with envy at this tissue of betweens, this braid of breathings
which is air, from its own point,
fixed at the beginning, or the end?

Pigeons V'ed up into the warm wind everyone
was wary of, was waiting for the punch line —
we weren't born yesterday, you know — but the story
wavered, slowed,
this is where the lady in the pink hat crosses the park when
we want
to let go and weep with the streets and the shut
flat colours of the laneway
blush:
then everyone in the closet wants out,
baseball gloves, cherry-centred secrets,
rubber boots that squirm in their skins so
horny they say only foot foot puddle puddle while each
puddle
openly ogles, in deep focus,
a tangle of hydro wires and branches and,
way down there,
far below its concrete bottom,
sky.

SONG FOR BEEF CATTLE

To be whimless, o monks of melancholy,
to be continents completely
colonized, to stand
humped and immune, digesting,
redigesting our domestication, to be too too
solid flesh making its slow
progress toward fast food.
To feel our heavy heads becoming knock-knock jokes,
                                    who's there,
kabonk, Big Mac, to know our knees
are filled-in ampersands, things to fall on,
not run with.
To put all this to music — a bellow
which extinguishes the wolf, the long arc of its howl
reduced to gravity and spread,
ghostless, flatulent,
over the overgrazed acres.

The Ruffed Grouse cannot be seen unless you step inside its panic, and, since this must be done by accident, there is a certain stress involved. *Brambambambambam.* As though your poor heart hadn't enough to put up with, now it's exploded, like popcorn battering the lid with fluffy white fists. Simply ignore it. This was but a ruse to distract you from the grouse itself, as it flaps, an obese moth, further off into the under-brush. Notice instead the subtle blendings of bar and shade, everything ish, everything soft, the apotheosis of feather. But, as your heart can appreciate, its terror is a sumo wrestler.

It is easier to make one in your own yard. Just scrape together a clump of dead leaves about the size of a football. Add an elderberry for an eye, and squeeze together – not too hard, you don't want to wind up with a pigeon – as if you were making dough. Leave a small cavity for your secret fear. Cover and let stand. After an hour place it under a bush, turn your back, and – presto! – it's a clump of dead leaves again. But a clump of dead leaves capable of instant catastrophe. All your eggs in one basket.

If unknowing is a cloud, it must be elsewhere –
some baffled kingdom
where they clot in thickening air.
Here, in radical 3-D,
dangerous brains are hung against the sky, unembodied,
cumulative, Nietzschean,
making themselves up.
They cast their shadows on the crops,
they make the spruce sing sharp,
and scare the people into being weather wise,
watchful. Clarity
attends them and great weight
withheld. Oscar Peterson plays "In the Wee Small Hours"
with such softness in such power
and vice versa. Look:
here comes the camel, the whale, the kleenex, *l'oreiller
d'assassin*. Watch.
They signify all over the map
and do not fear to tread.

Can litheness lose itself but live
in memory, like a song
without its tune? She hunched herself
out of the maple bush, along its dappled,
freckled, nearly underwater path we watched her,
blue note after blue note,
make her way up to the porch. Thelonius Monk gets lost
somewhere around midnight, never getting past
11:45 and shuffling
brilliantly. Somebody dumped her. Somebody from town
for whom a sick cat was the final straw and now she'd
found our porch and one last chance
to make it back to catness from the bush of ghosts.
Now she must do the old seductive rub, must struggle to
                                                    leap
to the rail and stretch, must spread her claws, curl,
uncurl, lick her wrist,
and wash her face with it, yawn and paw at some
imaginary bug and make us think she was as smart
as Kit Smart's Jeoffry.

She was. Who's to say what kind of dance I'll manage
when the time comes, trailing tubes
and catheters, clutching my IV trolley as I
shimmy toward the exit?

II

SNOWLIGHT

Because the swallows had departed from the cliff,
over and over,
the soft knives of their wings tasting the river mist as they
went wherever it is
they went, because
with the air free of their chatter we could hear ourselves
think, because the notes
we left in their holes, full of love and envy
and lament, were never answered and because we need
an earth with ears to hear the long dread
carpentry of history, and then, and so, and so,
and then, each bone nailed, wired, welded,
riveted, because we knew
the gods we loved were charismatic fictions, and because
the swallows had departed.

KINDS OF BLUE #76 (EVENING SNOW)

A blue against the easy clarities of sky,
a blue that eats the light, a bruise

ascended from forgetfulness. Things
have been overtaken by their shadows, stilled

and stricken dumb. What did they know
anyway? Only cold may speak

or not speak. Inside pain,
singing, inside song

another pain which is the dialects of snow.
And us, full of holes

and chambers
and for rent.

First we feel it, trouble, trouble, our airspace
beaten by its own scared heart,
then spot the little bug-blot growing in the sky,
descending to the heliport.
We've all seen M*A*S*H,
those domesticated valkyries. Yet
it holds our ears and gazes, throbbing
like the heavy bass on someone else's amp as it
hovers, lowers as though trying to lay an egg,
carefully. See,
says a lady at the day care,
crouching by a child, someone sick
is coming to the hospital from way up north.
I'm paused beside them on the sidewalk,
thinking of Virginia Woolf – how she would
cherish this bouquet of looks, this small
figure in the infinite welter of mind –
until it drops from sight. Well.
It's the machines who will keep watch now, high
in those immaculate rooms, chirping and pinging
like kept birds, counting the atoms
as they fall.
       And the angel,
when it comes, may not announce itself
with any buffeting of ears,
may not even whisper,
may not even be a full-fledged angel, may be
just an eddy of the air, which
catches the stuttered heart in its two-step
and is off.

No fixed address.
In this ruined suburb, not much remains
upright. The doors, reciting names and numbers,
are still trying to impress upon eternity
the values of identity and neatness. Long since
the houses have collapsed into their basements.
Row after row, the crosses
commemorate the last right angles: farewell table,
friend to elbow and book, farewell calendar,
framer of days, goodbye bed,
you dreamboat, you playpen,
so long board games on the carpet,
so long carpet
               so long boards. Final score
Snakes 11   Ladders 0.

You can see what must be happening back home.
She has opened the door to let leaves blow
into the kitchen.
               She lets beautiful blue
snowlight fill the uncurtained rooms.

there was no place we could sit or look
that was not changed to an icon, cursed
with significance: the clothes tree
groping air, the last video, her fish still
nosing the glass, the clocks,
which might as well be moons, the beds,
mouths, and the great great
grandmother staring bleakly from her portrait.
It is just what she might have suspected.

Suddenly at home the cigarette replaces sentences,
its red eye burning in.
In each phrase
the blessèd finch of small talk perishes.
What can you say,
we say, it will take
time, we say, while the mills of thought churn
should have should have and the dog
holds everyone under suspicion.

GRIEF AND THE SEA

The sea as it spends itself
can teach us how to grieve – the way
it rushes onto a rock beach, seethes
and sucks back, informationless
                              the way
it booms under a cliff,
calling all things to their hollows.

Then the 3% of body which is solid
wishes it weren't. The sad
shopping cart of the mind imagines
dumping its confections.
It would rather be a trellis.
It would rather be a net with fifty-foot holes,
an unplayed game of tic tac toe.

The pull of the grave is mute, and leads
straight to a mouthful of clay.
But the sea grieves with the moon's
slim gravity
and tugs your loss into its own
insinuating music.

RAIN, RAIN, RAIN

On the roof its drone
is the horizon drawing closer for a
kiss, for an embrace whose message is,
whose muscle is the comfort of,
the family of,
the sociability of being mortal.

Outside, the leaves have multiplied its pitter
into the stuff of plainsong.
So many oceans to be spoken of.
Such soft ovations numbering
innumerable names for hush.
Who understands this tongue? No one.
No one and no one and no one.

In thin

mountain air, the single note

lives longer, laid along its

uninflected but electric, slightly

ticklish line, a close

vibrato waking up the pause

which follows, then

once more on a lower or a higher pitch and

in this newly minted

interval you realize the wilderness

between one breath

and another.

For the following few seconds, while the ear
inhales the evening
only the offhand is acceptable. Poetry
clatters. The old contraption pumping
iambs in my chest is going to take a break
and sing a little something. What? Not much. There's
a sorrow that's so old and silver it's no longer
sorry. There's a place
between desire and memory, some back porch
we can neither wish for nor recall.

Because my heart has never been in love with pumping
but with blood, its song goes
                              river river river
a song like spending money I can ill afford,
like bleeding, sung beneath its strict, beneath its
closely monitored metrics you can hear it going doctor
doctor when I watch this water, whipped
and brimming, all its colours
trying to talk at once, I get this feeling like a
fist, like watching a mob scene on the TV news you know
they're going to snap shut like a purse,
like a proverb, suddenly
shouting some deplorable truth
in unison.

THE LAUGH

> "The inverse of language is like a laughter that
> seeks to destroy language, a laughter infinitely
> reverberated."
> — Emmanuel Levinas

The laugh that ate the snake and
runs through the city dressed in a sneeze, the mischief
done in these sly
passages of time, when the tongue is
severed from the voice and
fed to the weather, when the running
patter of catbirds simply
swallows the agenda, nothing to be held back,
nothing rescued in a catch-phrase or figure, your
house is on fire
and your children are gone.
When evenings pass as unseen
immaculate ships, and folk –
everyone is suddenly folk – rush to their porches
and lift their faces to this
effervescence of air,
wishing.
        Wishing what?
Just wishing.

After the aesthetic poverty, the bonhomie,
bravado, after the melodies which swell and
spread themselves like easy money,
no one pays the bill
and Mimi dies on four blasts from the horns.
Death is outside in his pickup
which is like a rock. C'mon Mimi
for chrissake.
Now what, brave
bohemians, with the century down to its last
evocative cough and bad
inflammable manuscript,
and an ocean of cold hands rising in the streets?

WHAT KIND OF FOOL AM I?

Bill Evans Solo Sessions 1963

To find your way through the
phrase. Some keys are made of edges some
of broken glass. Bauble. Bangle. You knew the tune
before it was mined. You are the kind of fool
who searches through the rubble of his favourite
things. A note could fall in love off
a cliff down a well. When you fall
it will be forever. Whoever has no house whoever
picks his way and finds
his favourite ledge. Far from April,
far from Paris. Far from his left hand down there
pecking the bright shiny beads. Telling them
off. That kind of fool. Everything
happened to you.

So, you are saying, it comes
to this – the end of voice, swan songs
in the can:
>   all that singing in the shower,
>   all that palaver, sweet talk, sales pitch, I-don't-
>   want-to-walk-without-you-
>   babies; pillow talk's soft
>   husky bottoms, phone calls breaking talk down
>   into particles which
>   blossom in the ear, the mike
>   like a svengali saying *be*
>   *voluptuous, be public*; and the quick
>   soprano silver that was glance,
>   was wing, that would turn transparent air
>   into a mirror, and transcend the phlegm – to this,
you say,
this heaviness
this mute weight in your hands.

Now you hope, having combed,
as the expression goes, the slopes,
and spent enough to underwrite a middle-sized crusade,
for evidence: catches, flaws,
the return of surly bonds – the facts
which can only add up.
>   But think of your inklings,
how they grew, inking in whole
corners. How Frankie loved Johnny.
Think of that shade behind the beat,
the jazz lag which,

by being barely place, is most so:
the patch of anonymous ground where all our failures meet
to grow alliterative with rust, where the voice
keeps its desire to eat dirt.
To every thing

there was a season. To every melody a door
at which we pause and want to stay paused – surely your hand
has rested on the latch?
Now think of us as falling,
as dusk does, sideways, and not through that door
but into it –

        the butts of slapstick.
That was the lick we never knew.
That was the horse laugh lurking in the surface.

> "Maybe it is a good idea for us to keep a few
> dreams of a house that we shall live in later, always
> later, so much later, in fact, that we shall not have
> time to achieve it."
>
> — Gaston Bachelard, *The Poetics of Space*

Shakes, lord it
shakes like an eardrum with every bomb-
blast in this ongoing
artificial war. Just the same
it sails the gravel ridge, brow held high,
like its builder, Captain Weston,
who beheld the river from its third-floor belvedere:
one foot in the afterlife,
as dreamt by the nineteenth century, one in oblivion
as realized in ours.

Who would live here?
                    Fools,
fools like us, from away, who fall
for its wide maritime windows like a kind
of candour, its nooks
like a kind of wit. Fools who see themselves
as captains of whatever, writing in a high place
or sleeping under a tin roof that reflects the stars
and amplifies the rain.
Who maunder, room to shaken room,
listening for something.
As though the old house tried and tried
for a ghost of its own but had its concentration

broken. The curse
died in the chimney. No illicit kiss.
The axe stayed in the shed.
                              Only the fools walk,
heads at an angle,
through its generous unbalanced spaces.

                    *

It spoke directly from the nooks of revery, easily bypassing
everything we'd ever learnt. As though the solitudes lived in
by the writing mind, usually represented, chastely, by a
particular cushion and chair, had grown from perches into
potential habitations. Up top, the lookout ("belvedere" came
from the worlds of cigarettes and fashion) was both den and
weather-eye. "Womb with a view," I joked; later an extra
strong concussion cracked a pane. An elfin, irresistible door-
way led to a low loft over the kitchen where the windows
came nearly to the floor. Out back, a drive-shed had been
turned into a workshop, then a pottery, then back into a
workshop. Now it had a solid bench and a pot-bellied stove,
affable as an uncle. The ground-floor bathroom had once
served as the village post office, before the days of the base,
when the village had been a village with two general stores
and a blacksmith. We browsed between shy spaces, imagin-
ing a lamp, a corner table, a rug, and shelves, shelves,
shelves. This was not a good frame of mind from which to
shop, one full metamorphosis removed from real estate, with
its problematic of plumbing and heating, and, in this case,
simulated warfare. Later we came to realize that spaces such
as this cannot not listen; they are inner ears whose power lies
in their complete susceptibility to tremor.

Is language the house of being, as Heidegger claims? Or is the house of being simply a house – the one that haunts you from the future, with its porch, its nooks, its path dawdling off into the birches? The one you dwell toward and mustn't catch; the one where you will always play the fool.

III

MATÉRIEL

(i) THE MAN FROM NOD

Since his later history is so obscure, it's no wonder he is most remembered for his first bold steps in the areas of sibling rivalry and land use. It should not be forgotten that, although Adam received God's breath, and angels delivered his message, it was Cain who got tattooed – inscribed with the sign which guarantees a sevenfold revenge to be dished out to antagonists. Sometimes translated "Born to Lose."

He was the first to realize there is no future in farming.

How must he have felt, after tilling, sowing, weeding, harvesting, and finally offering his crop, about God's preference for meat? Was God trying to push his prized human creatures further into the fanged romance of chasing and escaping? Was he already in the pocket of the cattle barons? Cain must have scratched and scratched his head before he bashed in his brother's.

He becomes the first displaced person, exiled to the land of Nod, whose etymology, as he probably realized, was already infected with wandering. Then his biography goes underground, rumouring everywhere. Some say he tries farming once again in the hinterland, scratching illegibly at the glacial till before hitting the first road. Some say he fathers a particularly warlike tribe, the Kenites. Some, like Saint Augustine, claim that he takes revenge on agriculture by founding the first cities, rationalizing all his wanderings into streets and tenements, and so charting the course for enclosures and clearances to come. But perhaps his strategy is simpler and more elegant. Perhaps he just thins into his anger, living as a virus in the body politic: the wronged assassin, the antifarmer, the terrorist tattooed with the promise of sevenfold revenge. Like anyone, he wants to leave his mark.

Atrocity
implies an audience of gods.
The gods watched as swiftfooted
godlike Achilles cut behind the tendons of both feet
and pulled a strap of oxhide through
so he could drag the body of Hektor,
tamer of horses, head down in the dust
behind his chariot.
Some were appalled, some not,
having nursed their grudges well, until
those grudges were fine milkfed
adolescents, armed
with automatic weapons. The gods,
and farther off,
the gods before the gods, those who ate
their children and contrived
exquisite tortures in eternity, watched
and knew themselves undead. Such is the loss, such
the wrath of swiftfooted godlike
Achilles, the dumb fucker, that he drags,
up and down, and round and round the tomb
of his beloved, the body of Hektor,
tamer of horses. Atrocity
is never senseless. No. Atrocity is dead ones
locked in sense, forbidden
to return to dust, but scribbled in it,
so that everyone – the gods,
the gods before the gods, the enemy, the absent mothers, all
must read what it is like to live out exile on the earth
without it, to be without recesses, place,

a campsite where the river opens
into the lake, must read
what it means to live against the sun and not to die.
Watch,
he says, alone in the public
newscast of his torment, as he
cuts behind the tendons of both feet,
and pulls a strap of oxhide through,
so he can drag the body that cannot stop being Hektor,
tamer of horses, head down in the dust
behind his chariot, watch
this.

(iii) THE BASE

Unheard helicopter chop
locks my mind in neutral.
What was it I was supposed to think
as I entered the forbidden country of the base? For this
was not the wisdom I had bargained for –
banality. No orchids of evil
thriving on the phosphorus that leaks
from unexploded shells. No litter of black
ratatats like insoluble hailstones, or fungi
springing up from dead ka-booms.
After nearly forty years of shattered air, I find
not one crystal in the khaki gravel.
Nondescription.

What was Cain thinking
as he wandered here? Whatever
"here" may be, for it has largely been forgotten
by the maps, and also by itself, a large anonymous
amnesia in the middle of New Brunswick.
What shapes occupied the mind
which since has occupied the landscape?
Did he foresee this triumph of enchantment
whereby place itself becomes its camouflage,
surrenders Petersville, Coot Hill and New
Jerusalem, to take up orders?
Did he anticipate the kingdom of pure policy,
whose only citizens – apart
from coyotes, ravens, moose –
are its police?
Except for graveyards, which have been

preserved, this real estate is wholly owned
and operated by the will, clearcut,
chemicalled and bombed.
Black wires like illegible writing
left everywhere. Ballistics? Baker Dog Charley?
Plastic vials tied to trees at intervals, containing
unknown viscous liquid. In some folktale
I can't conjure, I would steal this potion
and confer great gifts – or possibly destruction –
upon humanity. In a myth
or Wonderland, I'd drink it and become
a native. No thanks.

                    Yet blueberries grow, creeks
sparkle, and an early robin
sings from the scrub. Can a person eat
the berries when they ripen? What kind of fish
thicken in the creeks? During hunting season,
claims the Base Commander, moose and deer
take sanctuary in the impact areas, since no personnel
may enter. Often, late September, you may
see a moose, Jean Paul L'Orignal, perhaps,
sitting on a stump along the border of the base,
huge chin resting on a foreleg,
pondering alternatives: cheerful psychopaths
in psychedelic orange, or a moose-sized replica
of the absurd, ka-boom?

Now I recall
the story of the soldier detailed to attack
an "enemy position," which turned out to be
his grandfather's old farmhouse. Basic Training:
once out of nature he was not about
to get sucked in by some natural seduction

and disgrace himself with tears
or running to the kitchen for an oatmeal cookie.
He made, as we all do, an adjustment.
                                    Standing here
still parked in neutral
I'm unable to identify the enemy's position or
sort the evil genii from fallen
farmers, victims and assassins
interpenetrate with vendors and *vendus* in long
chromosomal threads.
                              Time to retreat.
Walking back, I try to jump a creek
and sprain my wrist. Pick up your god-damned
feet —. Still, I stop to cut two
pussy willow branches. Why? Imagined
anti-fasces? Never
was the heaviness of gesture
heavier, nor hope more of a lump,
than trying to imagine that those buds
might, back home in the kitchen, unclench, each fragile hair
pom-pommed with pollen, some day
to open into leaf.

(iv) *STRETTO*

Having oversold the spirit, having,
having talked too much of angels, the fool's rush, having the
                                                                    wish,
thicker than a donkey's penis,
holier than o, having the wish
to dress up like the birds,
to dress up like the birds and be and be and be.
Off the hook.
Too good for this world.
Unavailable for comment.
Elsewhere.

                    *

                    Wonderful Elsewhere, Unspoiled,
Elsewhere as Advertised, Enchanted, Pristine,
Expensive. To lift, voluptuous, each feather cloak
worth fifty thousand finches: to transcend
the food chains we have perched upon and hover – hi there
fans from coast to coast –to beam back dazzling
shots of the stadium, drifting in its cosmos
like a supernova, everywhere the charged
particles of stardom winking and twinking, o, exponentially
us. As every angel is.

                    *

                    Every angel is incestuous.
Agglutinoglomerosis: the inlet choked with algae thriving on
                                        the warmth

imparted by the effluent. *Contermitaminoma*: runoff through
the clearcut takes the topsoil to the river then
out into the bay to coat the coral reef in silt. *Gagaligogo*:
seepage from the landfill finds the water table. *Elugelah*: the
                                                    south-
sea island angelized by the first H-blast.
                                    In the dead sea
we will float as stones. Unmortal

                    *

                            Unmortality Incorporated.
No shadow. All day
it is noon it is no one. All day
it utters one true sentence jammed
into its period. Nothing is to be allowed
to die but everything gets killed
and then reclassified: the death of its death
makes it an art form. Hang it.
Prohibit the ravens. Prohibit the coyotes.
Prohibit the women with their oils and cloths and
weep weep weeping. Tattoo this extra letter
on the air:
            This is what we can do.
Detonation. Heartbeats of the other,
signed, sealed,
delivered. Thunder
eats of its echo eats its vowels smothers its
elf. To strike
hour after hour   the same hour. To dig
redig the gravels that are no one's grave.

                    *

Gravels, aye, tis gravels ye'll gnash mit muchas gracias and will it please thee sergeant dear to boot me arse until I hear the mermaids sinking? You know it: tis the gravel of old rocknroll highroad, me darling sibs, the yellow brick jornada del muerto. You fancy me far from your minds, wandering lonely as a clod in longlost brotherhood, while your door's locked and your life's grammatically insured, yet (listen) *scurry scurry* (Is–that–Only–A–Rat–In–The–Basement–Better–Phone–Dad–Oh–No–The–Line's–Dead, Mandatory Lightning Flash) yup, here I am with the hook old chum. Hardly Fair, what? Now gnash this: beautiful tooth, tooth beautiful. Repeat: die nacht ist die nacht. How many fucking times do I have to *Fucking* tell you, me rosasharns? Nayther frahlicher ner mumbo, nayther oft when on my couch I lie ner *bonny doom* will lift from these eyes of thine their click clock particles of record time. *Ammo ergo somme*. We bombs it back to square one, then, o babes in arms, we bombs square one. Nomine Fat Boy ate Elugelah ate Alamogordo gravel. Mit click clock lock licht nicht. Encore.

Die Nacht ist die Nacht.

IV

THREE ECLOGUES

(i) SUNDAY MORNING, RAISIN RIVER

The citizens are sleeping or in church, their outboards
snugged into the bank, each prow
pointing to its Private sign. We slide upriver,
past the Evinrudes and Mercs, the cottages with lawns
right down to the water. To own, to mow.
To say the same river, the same river,
who can blame us?
Only from some prospect like Intensive Care,
or a canoe, does slippage
sing in the veins. This morning
I want to be in my wrists
listening to the slow
urge of current, feeling it erode,
feeling the canoe give way
to make it. Further on
the lawns give way to the scruff of habitat.
Think how a reed or stick
can turn into a Great Blue Heron lifting off
as dusk would, if it rose. And that inner wing
opening – sympathetic magic – how
it's too large for your chest, and useless, an umbrella
in a closet. In my bestiary of extinctions, hope,
earth's angel, is a heron.
Around the next bend, something nasty
seizes the breeze. Shit passed through a pulp mill? No, just
automated pig barn: in that book of beasts
I'll need a place for ownership made absolute – reaching
after death and through the multiple
humiliations of the flesh. A simple grid should do,
                                            supplemented

(if we get the funding) with a patch of scratch 'n' sniff.
Now, Barnswallows skirl,
skim, kiss, the death of the bug   .
a pucker on the surface. Blue Vervain
                    Joe Pye Weed
                    Autumn Wild Onion on the banks
Arrowhead among the reeds. Then one whole stretch
covered in Wild Grape, looping limb to stem to
fallen log, tapestry
and jungle. *Rivière Raisin*: are these the vines,
or their descendants, which inspired the name?
Imagine those first voyageurs
happening upon a free-form vineyard, *sacré bleu*,
their paddles momentarily suspended, dripping.
Imagine the huge cedars, oak, pine
(now beams and floors in Williamstown)
reaching up to drink the light, and down,
their roots like many-fingered hands to hold the soil
that fed them. How should they
be represented? At the centre let's include
a signature of empty pages – not
the blue and blue-grey white of winter but the speckled
off-white of amnesia. A clearance. Or –
print all pages as before but leave the whole
unbound. We turn downriver as the first launch,
with its happy family, throbs around the bend.
Sister has remembered the boom-box,
which nicely complements the horsepower.
And let the fly leaf read
This Book Shall Be My Trees.

(ii) ON FOOT TO THE BYPASS ESSO POSTAL OUTLET

As I walk to the Bypass Esso Postal Outlet
a raven crosses my mind. So what? At this point
the Trans-Canada achieves four lanes – a big deal
in New Brunswick – as it takes the ridge in one
simplified glide. Beside me, eighteen-wheelers –
Laidlaw, Midland, Day and Ross – always on the verge
of catching and devouring the future,
spend their momentum and are forced to downshift,
wrathfully. They've been everywhere
and boxed it, they've been hauling all the way
from depots in the late Cretaceous, they pay
millions in taxes and will make Halifax tonight.
Walking in their outwash, I'm dismissed. I think of the guy
I used to pass as I drove from house to job,
walking the shoulder with his eye on the ditch, angular,
nearly metronomic, shopping bags bobbing.
After a month or so
I thought of him as Charlie Chaplin's twin, the sinister
unfunny one, trapped in that silent movie.
                                        Out here I realize
more about the workings of the engine, how it sheds its pain –
or is that ecstasy – shouting hush hush hush,
dividing life into combustion and exhaust, how you
have to eat that. In the ditch, jetsam: plastic allsorts,
chrome, styrofoam like pasteurized snow, cups from
Tim Hortons, one sneaker,
the bottles and cans he collected
to cash in. Down the slope, The View:
                                        the river,

snaking between humpbacked hills, looking like the official
                                                    logo
for The River Valley Trail, which calls Come Home
to tourists, leading the eye into the middle distance
where the hills fold into one another: Mom.
                                        If I weren't
taking the mail to the postal outlet I might
cross the highway and walk into them – up the muddy lane
past the abandoned appliances (the dryer arse up,
airing its vent like a baboon) past the deeryard and the little
                                                    waterfall
to the lookout over Garden Creek.
There I would watch for ravens and the improbable
Pileated Woodpecker, and listen for the tinkering of
                                        kinglets. Once
I walked up here among their miniature bells,
which later on turned out to be the change
jingling in my pocket.
                        But today I'm on the bypass
when a raven crosses my mind. Imagine an animated
Chinese character, one element of which is roadkill,
one the gravel underneath, and one
the radical of chance. To be that style,
to utter raucous introverted music which will carry over
                                                    hills
and under traffic, to draw close to your ear
and whisper its horizon note. To lose it, tumbling out of
                                        thought,
gone gaga, then
find the wind under my wing and away.
I think there is a secret shelf, left empty,
where language goes to fray back into air.
That's where I imagine

talking with a raven about whatever
happened to be happening – the late spring, the playoffs,
conspicuous and inconspicuous consumption, the
                                                importance
of the Trans-Canada as provider of dead meat.
We'd turn phrases then,
turn them over to see what was crawling
underneath, we'd throw our voices to the winds
from whom we'd borrowed them.
At the Bypass Esso I will
post this batch of poems, hoping for the small
matter-of-fact miracle of ears.
Will there be that other to whom,
suddenly, they find themselves addressed?
Maybe not. Next door, Tim Hortons
where the mounties go for coffee.
Maybe I will join them. Or
maybe I will find myself back out here with the traffic,
picking up popcans,
listening for the moment when a raven takes a piece of sky,
packs it like a snowball,
and speaks.

As always, I walk the ties, trying to
syncopate my step to their awkward
interval. It's hot. At some age, six or eight,
the distance matches the length of your leg exactly,
you can march to town in two-four time. Now
Cow Vetch and Mustard get in the way
and hide the ties. "Sleepers." Watch your step.
A Goldfinch lands on a rail, then a White-tail Dragonfly,
its pause a half-beat between darts. The heat
is tired in its bones, exhausted by absent thunder
like a couple trying to get pregnant, dragging their sad
much-discussed ass to bed.
Back in Moderns, Dr. Reaney led us
into Yoknapatawpha County. He had been there.
                                                  "Remember
it is *hot*; stick all that past in a pot
and set it on the stove." Bindweed and Wild Grape
curl around the rails, tendrils, tentacles, the tracks
in the distance with their old
Parkinsonian shake. Around my head
the comic-book sign for dizziness is being etched
by deerflies. Quentin Compson
hungers for his sister, who will later bear a daughter,
also Quentin, who will steal the cash,
her own, from her ordinary, evil
uncle, and run off with the red-tied carny-man. Hawkweed
                                                  and Daisies
sharpen their hardihood on gravel. The spikes,
once hammered like cold bolts from the blue,

are loosening. Feel this —
a wobbly tooth. We loved the old train, really, it
would take an afternoon's mosquito and cicada hum,
pre-amplify it, put a big bass underneath, we'd feel it
in the air the way, I guess, a horse can sense an earthquake
                                        coming, we'd
drop everything – berry pails, books – and run down
to the tracks, Luke in manic overdrive because
June was busting out all over and we'd all turned dog.
                                        We'd stand
throbbing in its aura, waving; the blunt-faced locomotive,
a few tanker cars full of polysyllabic stuff,
the caboose with maybe a reciprocating wave, the throb
thinning to the whine of iron wheels on iron rails.
To be next door to violence, that dreadful
blundering. It was fun. It was cathartic. Now it's like
single-point perspective had let go, shattering into the tip
tilt hop of the Yellow Warbler's pointillist attention
in the Rock Elm. So much intricate
tenacity. Milkweed with its lavish
muted blooms, the milk that feeds the larvae
of Monarch Butterflies and makes them
poisonous to birds. When the train ran over Luke
it was too dumb to pause or blow its whistle, probably
never saw him there between the tracks or heard us
shouting into the electric deafness of the moment.
Well. That spot is occupied by Bladder Campion now.
With its cheeks puffed out behind its blooms, it's like
a gang of Dizzy Gillespies and the final
freeze-frame for the story: except, somehow
Luke survived the train, and then the shock,
which also should have killed him.

Back from the vet, stitched,
still groggy from the drugs, he sensed the old throb
troubling the air and struggled growling to his feet
ready for round two. Talk about dumb. It was funny
and appalling, and we knew, wincing at each other,
that it wasn't just our true intrepid friend
we were appalled by. When the Monarchs hatch
they'll feed and flit and pollinate their hosts,
by accident, and after an infinitude of flits
wind up precisely in one Mexican valley. Some thoughts
live in the mind as larvae, some as the milk they feed on,
some as the wanderings which are the way. Heal-all,
Yarrow. Everything the tracks
have had no use for's happening
between them.

V

TO DANCELAND

MEDITATION ON ANTIQUE GLASS

This room, whose windows are waterfalls
in stasis, dreaming in one place, is wrong
for figuring your income tax or poker.
Susceptibility
they say as they teach the light to cry
and introduce hard facts to their first
delicious tremors of metamorphosis:
susceptibility
as though the film were paused at the point of flashing back,
woozy with semiosis: *the rapids are gentle*,
they say, *drink me*. Wrong
for marking essays or making plans.

Nights are worse. Darkness,
as it makes love to the glass, grows thick
and rich, advertising for itself, it whispers
memory muscle, whispers
Guinness is good for you, whispers
loss is its own fur, whispers
once, once
irresistibly.

ODE TO MY CAR

As if. As if it oiled your idle
notions, machined,
massaged them till there never was no
clunk no hand me that spanner no
crank 'er over.
As if motor were simply the syrinx of speed as if
movie movie all you ever have to pay is your attention,
                                        focus
on the docudrama in the windshield, stay tuned
to the hummingbird who hums in the accelerator, in
                                    the cylinders
the six brave heart attacks are singing and the clutch
performs the sigh with which the lovers shift into
                                 more comfortable
positions:
        there.
Something has come from nothing, as if
a handful of its blackberries had been
gathered. Something in a tooth
desires to speak in tongues. Something in a consonant
attends its vowels, as if
minuet. Synchromesh.
Momentum. Here lies the precise
mystery of transmission.

DUBBIN

It is natural to do it by a fire
and it is natural to hum,
but not to sing. The leather
speaks back to your fingers, an old hand
to a young one, already comforting your corpse
while you recall its ghost, rubbing in animal fat,
working the worklines from your boots until
the dusk returns to the surface. Kingtread —
undead once again.

And the fingers?
As a kid, I dubbined my baseball glove
religiously, massaging the pocket,
the web. Tallowed.
Sort of daydream, sort of foreplay,
sort of summoning. Summoning?
There would be a peaked pure moment when,
deep in the hole at short,
it would pick an impossible liner from the air,
Black Diamond The Animal Hand.
                              Or, better yet,
to wake one night from the dark recurrent dream
to find it on the bedpost,
whiskered and snorting,
a goggle-eyed fish in its paws.

The tools of music: this is where it first
emerged from noise and how it
stays in touch with clutter
and how it gets back to the heart –
that single-stroke kachunker with its grab, give,
grab. He is bringing the kitchen,
the workshop, screwing wingnuts and attaching
brackets, placing the pedals like accelerators,
setting up the stands for snare and high hat like decapitated
wading birds. How music will make itself walk
into the terrible stunned air behind the shed
where all the objects looked away. Now the hollow bodies,
their blank moons tilted *just asking for it*, and back and
back to the time you missed the step
and dropped the baby and your heart leapt out
to catch it, for all those accidents that might have
and that happened he floats the ride and then
suspends the crash above the wreckage like its flat
burnished bell.
Unsheathes the brushes that can shuffle through the grass
or pitter like small rain. All this hardware to recall
the mess you left back home
and bring it to the music
and get back to the heart.
He sits on the stool
in the middle of your life
and waits to feel the beat. To speak it
and keep it. Here we go.

"Their behaviour is acoustically mysterious . . . we get fundamentals being pitched a third or a fourth deeper, as if the air column were projected back, in imagination, to the true apex of the cone-bore, which is in most cases several inches beyond the reed (down the player's throat, as it were)."
— Anthony Baines, *Woodwind Instruments and Their History*

Lying in its case, the alto sax looks brash, *nouveau riche*, a gold tooth. Pick it up, heft it, plonk the keys down with a sound like whumping the top of a beer bottle. You could play this thing, man, it's just a kazoo with buttons. Follow the action as you press this key or that, watching the force reverse over a see-saw hinge or torque around the cylinder to pop a hole open or closed: *mechanism*: it's a fantastic insect, the elegance of niftiness rather than refinement. So blow. The sax isn't going to transform your breath like other instruments but magnify it, reaching back down your throat to amplify its possibilities, giving prominence to neglected dialects like the honk, the cough, the hum, and even (Archie Shepp) the last gasp. It does not concern itself with angels, as the flute, nor with the dead like Dante, modernism, and the cello. It does not even imitate or extend the human voice as the violin is said to do. The sax is equipment singing – our equipment: a troubling of air which addresses us, the dying, from our own respiratory systems. Its idiom is breath, unrelieved of the deplorable burdens of sex and work. It has the richness of a muffler in its last days, an overloaded ferry on a muddy river. You may hear your father's phlegmy old

Chev or the soft honk of Trumpeter Swans over miles of high prairie. You may hear *soupe du zoo*. You will always hear the sob in the note, the hollow sob which comes from the lung, the womb of voice. The sob that will gather the unsayable without cashing it in on lyric silver. When the wind blows (Lao-tzu) there is only wind. When the sax blows there is only wind and the whole goddamned human condition. Mortality's exhaust pipe. Ready for nothing.

(i) *He rides into town*

already perfect, already filled with nothing. His music is a
hawk scream which has been crossed with a machine,
perhaps eternity's lathe, and fashioned into a horse. His
hatbrim is horizon. It is all over. Only the unspeakable
trauma which erased his name concerns him. Now it
concerns the townsfolk as they scuttle, gutless, behind
shopfronts. Two minutes ago their houses were three-
dimensional and contained kitchens, not to mention closets.
Now the houses, the general store, livery and sheriff's office
are so obviously props that the townsfolk have stopped
believing in them before the curtains twitch back into place.
Now they are cover awaiting shootout, and the townsfolk are
extras waiting to fall, aaargh, from their roofs, and crash,
spratinkle tinkle tinkle, through their windows. He rides into
town from another genre, from the black star that sucks the
depth from everything, a soundless bell tolling. *You should
have changed your life*, it says, *done, done, done*. Doesn't even
consider that you fixed up the den and took that night class in
creative writing.

(ii) *Their eyes meet*

ah, and there is a satisfying drag on the sprockets, as though
the celluloid were suddenly too heavy to turn, as though the
projector were sleepy. One violin has been stricken and
starts, legato, a drugged smoke alarm, to troll the theme,
which the camera catches, tracking left (always left) to take
in a quiver of lips. Close-up, close-up, two-shot, their four
eyes have begun to unbutton and bud, the strings now ahum,
vibrato, zoom zoom zoom they shed the depth of field. Who
needs it? The darkness is inhabited, the popcorn is buttered.
Their lips approach like shy cats. Her eyes have decided to
skinny-dip in his and his in hers: one more microzoom and
they dive, leaving the rest of their faces behind to nuzzle and
rub, attempting to smudge the irregular line between them.
And the eyes? Are swimming with us, dolphins, in the
darkness, which is rich and viscous, the lake of tears we've
been waiting for.

(iii) *We take our seats*

and settle into our bodies, waiting for the lights to dim so we can feel ourselves falling, this is the best part, feel ourselves falling into a safer kind of sleep, an elaborate parkland of carefully prepared surprises. As the curtains begin to part, *lingerie*, we can see through them to the screen, which has begun to flicker into being. Will the plot matter? Of course not. Movies have been sent to us to make up for the bathroom mirror, with its rigid notion of representation, and the family, with its chain-link semantic net. Here we feel ideas wriggle into costume and images reach toward us out of light. Soon their logos will appear – the winged horse in the symmetrical cosmos, perhaps, or shifting constellations that swirl into an O. Everything will be incarnate, *in camera*, anything can be a star.

Once home from the supermarket
(on special) they are Too Much,
red's own red, the red that says
it would rather be red, then dead,
than anything in between.
They spike the air
exploding into softness,
waking the kitchen to its myths – the table
sinks into its grain, the forks imagine claws,
the plastic shopping bags embrace eternal
returnability.

Our hearts honk.
Oh, we say, oh – as though
meeting our cuts and bruises in their afterlives, grown
perfect and articulate – oh: the sum
of yelps and sighs as white
is every colour in a chord.
                              I see Blurt
among them, also Clot, also Exit Wound,
the badge of factions.
And Fist, turned thoughtful, not
the famous knuckle ridge but hand's desire
to close around its darkness and grow dense.
Then innerness past intimacy –
labyrinths of lips
                    wombs
                         viscera
tabu.
And tucked behind,

still lurking in its sepals, Buddy the brave one,
the one who whispers, hey
pucker up.

SETTING THE TABLE

(i) Knife

who comes to the table fresh
from killing the pig, edge
of edges,
entry into zip.
                    Knife
who can swim as its secret
through the dialogue or glimmer
in a kitchen drawer. Who first appeared
in God's hand to divide
the day from the night, then the sheep
from the goats, then from the other
sheep, then from their comfortable
fleeces. Nothing sinister in this except
it had to happen and it was the first
to have to. The imperative
mood. For what we are about to take
we must be grateful.

(ii) Fork

a touch of kestrel,
of Chopin, your hand with its fork
hovers above the plate, or punctuates
a proposition. This is the devil's favourite
instrument, the fourfold
family of prongs: Hard Place,
Rock, Something You Should Know,
and For Your Own Good. At rest,
face up, it says,
please, its tines
pathetic as an old man's fingers on a bed.
Face down it says
anything that moves.

(iii) Spoon

whose eloquence
is tongueless, witless, fingerless,
an absent egg.
Hi Ho, sing knife and fork, as off they go,
chummy as good cop and bad cop,
to interrogate the supper. Spoon waits
and reflects your expression,
inverted, in its tarnished moonlight. It knows
what it knows. It knows hunger
from the inside
out.

Every pause pauses in its own style. This guy is standing in the entryway, not far enough in to see the ice surface, brought up short by the scritching of blades on ice. It is one of those sudden slowings when inertia throws the load forward, and he is suddenly aware of its weight. Nothing, but nothing could have dragged him back here, are you kidding, this thing is so degenerate they're selling the degeneracy, pretty soon they'll have hockey cards replicating famous contracts and endorsements, they'll induct lawyers into the hall of fame. Nothing. So, here he is. He is here because of some ancient wish; he is here because he once wrote love poems, if you can believe this, using hockey images; he is here because his grown-up children, who live in Halifax and cheer for the Citadels, have been egging him on. He is abject and deserves everything he gets. Twenty years ago he would actually harangue his children on the sweet anguish of an artform not quite breaking out, while decent parents were taking their kids to Sunday School or at least discussing the world's great religions. He played a full season of basement hockey with his son, including Stanley Cup playoffs (original six) which was won, unfortunately, by the Boston Bruins. He talked aesthetics, ritual and myth, the almost offside pass, delay delay on the two-on-one, the unexpected perfect move, the shot that imitates the wingbeat rather than the hammer. See? His daughter reading through it, game after game, Judy Blume to J.D. Salinger, lifting her head mildly (o, did someone score?) as the crowd, including her nuclear family, went wild.

And this intimate scritching now, like the noise of an old phonograph needle that sits, humbly, this side of the melody it unlocks, a fierce delicate carving that makes everything fluid, an etching of feathers. It is the voice of a class learning to write using straight pens and inkwells. He decides maybe he should get a coffee before he finds his seat, but it is already too late: he will be in for everything.

He will be here for the Kentucky Fried Chicken Pepsi Poster Feature and the Ford Escort Shootout, week after week for the industrial-strength organ filling every niche with noise. He will be here when the plexiglass shatters, turning into a soft rain which falls into the laps of the first row. The team mascot, a life-sized stuffed animal, will perform tricks on an ATV between each period, and one game, two months from now, will toss a cheerful puck into the stands which cuts an inattentive elderly person over the eye. Still later, when the mascot falls off the Ford Escort, the human being inside will himself sustain a concussion.

The Zamboni will oval the ice 913 times. There will be 206 sudden sags in tension when a goalie takes a hummingbird out of the air, and everyone drifts, his coil relaxing to curl and countercurl, slowly eddying to the faceoff circle or the bench. There will be another style of pause when a defence-man waits with the puck behind the net while the wingers wind up, circling then criss-crossing, and the defenceman holds their strands in his head as, once on a porch in August, someone might have braided her sister's hair. Between games he will hold in his own head the feel of the thoughtful soft pass delivered in the middle of the rush, like the erotic gift of vulnerability.

During this bout of fandom he will come to understand the minions of gravity: the hook, the hold, the glove in the face, the clutch-each-other-in-the-dance-of-everything-that-holds-you-down-or-fucks-you-up; he will understand "nagging injury," he will know "can't buy a goal." Often he will embarrass his seat-mates with hoarse critical shouts – Having a nice *sleep*, Charron?, Heartbreak Hotel, goalie. If he should buy a 50-50 draw ticket between the first and second periods of the game against Moncton on January 23, he will miss winning $902 by only two digits. Meanwhile he will buy Fredericton Canadiens keychains, lighters, sweatshirts, even a cookbook with recipes (mostly barbecue) supplied by the players, and send them to his children in order to punish them. It is already too late. In his nightmares the organist attempts "Claire de lune."

TO DANCELAND

> "No one is ever happier than when they're dancing."
> — Margaret McKay

South through bumper crops we are driving to Danceland,
                                        barley
oats, canola, wheat, thick as a beaver pelt, but late, she said,
late, since June had been so cold already we were deep
in August and still mostly green so it was nip
and tuck with frost and somewhere between Nipawin and
                                Tisdale finally
I found the way to say, um, I can't dance
you know, I can't dance don't ask me
why I am driving like a fool to Danceland having flunked it
twenty-seven years ago in the kitchen where my mother,
bless her, tried to teach me while I passively resisted,
doing the jerk-step while she tried to slow, slow, quick quick
slow between the table and the fridge, her face fading
like someone trying to start a cranky Lawnboy
                                        nevertheless,
                        step by sidestep
we are driving down the grid, Swainson's hawks occurring
                                        every
thirty hydro poles, on average
                        to Danceland
where the dancefloor floats on rolled horsehair
and the farmers dance with their wives even though it is not
                                        Chicago
where the mirror ball blesses everyone with flecks from
                        another, less rigorous, dimension
where the Westeel granary dances with the weathervane,

the parent with the child, the John Deere with the mortgage
where you may glimpse occasional coyote lopes and
                              gopher hops
where the dark may become curious and curl one long arm
                              around us
as we pause for a moment, and I think about my mother
                              and her
wishes in that kitchen, then
we feed ourselves to the world's most amiable animal,
in Danceland.

ACKNOWLEDGEMENTS

Some of these poems first appeared in the following maga-
zines: *TickleAce*, *Pottersfield Portfolio*, *Windhorse*, *Quarry*, *Poetry
Canada Review*, *Brick*, *Grain*, and *The Malahat Review*.

My thanks for long-term listening to Roo Borson, Kim
Maltman, Tim Lilburn, Stan Dragland, and Jan Zwicky; also
to Stan for his editorial acuity and care, the famous "fine tooth
and comb." "Audience" is much more than who shows up.

Special thanks to Sabine Campbell of *The Fiddlehead* for
invaluable help in preparing the manuscript, and for being
the sustaining presence of the magazine that has itself
sustained so many writers by lending both mouth and ear.

"Setting Up the Drums" is for Andy Miller.

"To Danceland" is for my mother, Margaret McKay, with
belated apologies and thanks.

The poems in section II, "Snowlight," are in memory of
Jessica Naomi McKay Sharpe, 1980-1994.